A Dorling Kindersley Book

Text Christopher Maynard
Project Editor Caroline Bingham
Art Editors Sarah Thornton/Claire Penny
Deputy Managing Art Editor Jane Horne
Deputy Managing Editor Mary Ling
Production Ruth Cobb
Consultant Theresa Greenaway
Picture Researcher Tom Worsley

Additional photography by Jane Burton,
Frank Greenaway, Colin Keates, Dave King, Susannah Price,
James Stevenson, Harry Taylor

First published in Great Britain in 1997
by Dorling Kindersley Limited,
9 Henrietta Street, London WC2E 8PS
Visit us on the World Wide Web at http://www.dk.com

Reprinted 1997

A CIP catalogue record for this book is available from the British Library.

ISBN: 0-7513-5516-X

Colour reproduction by Chromagraphics, Singapore
Printed and bound in Italy by L.E.G.O.

The publisher would like to thank the following for their kind
permission to reproduce their photographs:

t top, b bottom, l left, r right, c centre, BC back cover, FC front cover

Bruce Coleman Collection: Alain Compost FC cb, 18-19c; **Robert
Harding Picture Library**: 14-15cb; **Natural History Photographic
Agency**: Michael Leach 15tr; **Pictures Colour Library**: 10-11cb; **Rex
Features**: 12-13c; **Tony Stone Images**: Horst Baender 7tr, G Brad Lewis
18bl, Bryn Campbell BC cb, 16-17c, Alain Compost 18cr, Robert Everts
17br, Darrell Gulin endpapers, David Higgs 8tl, John Lawrence 10tl, Mark
A Leman 20-21cb, Joseph Mcbride 8-9c, Philip and Karen Smith 19cr,
Larry Ulrich 13tr, World Perspectives 9tr; **Telegraph Colour Library**: FC
cl, BC cl, 5clb; **Zefa Pictures**: 6-7c, 14tl

Contents

WHY

do volcanoes erupt?

Questions children
ask about the Earth

DK

DORLING KINDERSLEY

London • New York • Stuttgart • Moscow

Seen from space, stars shine boldly. But starlight passes through a layer of air around the Earth before it reaches us. As this air moves, it makes the stars appear to twinkle.

Why is the Earth so blue?
From space the Earth appears as a big blue ball, smudged

twinkle?

Why do clouds float so high?
Clouds are made up of zillions of water droplets, each invisible to us and so light that they simply float in the air. Warmed by the Sun, these droplets rise high into the sky, like miniature hot-air balloons. Then they clump together to make clouds.

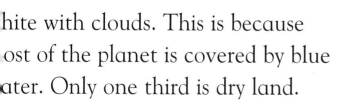

hite with clouds. This is because ost of the planet is covered by blue ater. Only one third is dry land.

Why do people# Why do people

We fall down, and not up, because of gravity. This force is created by the Earth, and it pulls everything very strongly down towards it. Without gravity, we would all float off into space.

Why can't we ski uphill?
It would be a funny sight if you whooshed uphill whenever you skied. You don't because gravity

fall downwards?

Why do astronauts float?
Astronauts are so high up, and travel so fast around the Earth that they escape Earth's pull of gravity. So in space they have no weight, and float. When they travel back to Earth, they fall to the ground under the force of gravity.

nly pulls one way – towards the centre f the Earth. That's why you slide down mountain and not up to the top.

The North and South Poles lie further from the Sun than any other places on Earth. Because sunlight is weak there, they stay cold all year round.

Why are there jungles?
Jungles need two things to thrive – lots of rain and lots of heat. At the equator, they get plenty of both. Here it rains almost every day, and in between the Sun blazes down. This is

icy at the Poles?

Why are there deserts?
Deserts are places that rain-bringing winds rarely reach. The rain may be blocked by mountains, so winds are often dry and suck up moisture. Really dry deserts may go as long as 20 years without rain.

n ideal environment for many
lants and animals
make
eir home.

When waves crash on to beaches they roll pebbles back and forth against

Why are cliffs dangerous?
A cliff face is unprotected from the effects of the sea, wind and rain. Under constant attack from these, it can weaken and may collapse. That's why it's never a good idea to stand right on the edge of a cliff.

smooth?

:ach other. After years of
ubbing, pebbles become
ounded and smooth.

Why is sand so soft?

A grain of sand is actually
as hard as a rock. But
because the grains are
so small, and the spaces
between them full of air
and water, they slide past
each other
smoothly and
feel soft to
walk on.

Why are there

Raindrops seep into the ground. If they find a soft rock called limestone, they eat away at it, forming little cracks

Why are there stalactites in caves?
Water drops leave tiny traces of a mineral called calcite on a cave's ceiling as they fall. Over thousands of years these accumulate, growing downwards like icicles, to form hanging shapes called stalactites.

caves?

...nd holes. In time, these
...row bigger and bigger,
...nd finally a cave is made.

Why do some animals live underground?

Animals such as badgers and rabbits like to burrow down into soil. A burrow makes a cosy shelter and is a safe place to run and hide from a predator such as a fox.

Oil is made from plants that were buried in mud on the sea bed millions of years ago. Eventually the mud changed to rock and the plants turned into the oil we now use for fuel.

Why do some rocks glitter?
Sometimes precious stones, called gems, are found in rocks. These are cut and polished to make them sparkle, then they are used for jewellery.

underground?

Why is gold so precious?

Gold is a pure yellow metal that occurs in thin seams in a rock called quartz. Gold never rusts, and it is so soft it can be worked into fine shapes. Gold is also very scarce, and this makes it valuable. It is widely used as a form of money.

Why do earthquakes

The Earth's crust is made of giant plates that move against each other. If the plates get stuck, pressure builds up. It is released when the plates finally slip. This release is in the form of an earthquake.

Why can't we dig through the Earth?
Deep underground there is so much pressure on rocks and soil that steel drills snap in two and holes close up as soon as they

18

happen?

...re dug. The very centre of ...he Earth is so hot that ...ocks melt. There is ...o way through.

Why does the earth crack?

If there is no rain for a long time, the ground begins to dry out as water turns into vapour and is carried away in the air. This is known as evaporation. Cracks appear as the earth tightens and shrinks.

Volcanoes exist at weak points in the Earth's crust. Active volcanoes act like giant plugs that hold back molten rock. Under this plug pressure builds up until, eventually, the volcano explodes.

Why does lava flow?
Lava is rock that is so hot it melts. It blasts out of volcanoes when they erupt.

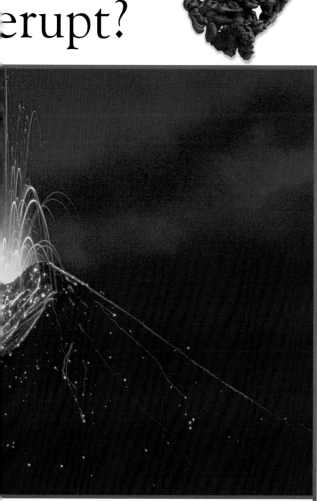

rming a burning orange river
fire. As soon as lava cools
wn it hardens, forming dozens
different types of rock.

Why are there mountains?

Mountains are like the rim of
a pie crust. While it only takes
fingers to mould pie crust,
the Earth's crust is shaped by
pressure on rocks deep within
the planet. The pressure
squeezes land together until it
rises up to form mountains.